POEMS **JASON PURCELL**

T0025745

swollening

ARSENAL PULP PRESS
VANCOUVER

SWOLLENING
Copyright © 2022 by Jason Purcell

ARSENAL PULP PRESS
Suite 202   211 East Georgia St.
Vancouver, BC V6A 1Z6
Canada
arsenalpulp.com

The publisher gratefully acknowledges the support of the Canada Council
for the Arts and the British Columbia Arts Council for its publishing
program, and the Government of Canada, and the Government of British
Columbia (through the Book Publishing Tax Credit Program), for its
publishing activities.

Arsenal Pulp Press acknowledges the xʷməθkʷəy̓əm (Musqueam),
Sḵwx̱wú7mesh (Squamish), and səl̓ilwətaʔɬ (Tsleil-Waututh) Nations,
custodians of the traditional, ancestral, and unceded territories where our
office is located. We pay respect to their histories, traditions, and continuous
living cultures and commit to accountability, respectful relations, and
friendship.

Cover and text design by Jazmin Welch
Cover art by Jazmin Welch
Edited by Joshua Whitehead
Proofread by Alison Strobel

Printed and bound in Canada

Library and Archives Canada Cataloguing in Publication:
Title: Swollening : poems / Jason Purcell.
Names: Purcell, Jason, author.
Identifiers: Canadiana (print) 20210385561 | Canadiana (ebook) 20210385588 |
   ISBN 9781551528854 (softcover) | ISBN 9781551528861 (HTML)
Classification: LCC PS8631.U736 S96 2022 | DDC C811/.6—dc23

CONTENTS

I

Things swallowed.

II

Sickness is not a metaphor.

III
If I had a window, it would be open.

I
Things swallowed.

I call you
my body to me—I think
I misplaced a memory, the past behind
the wall and rotting. Gagging
on childhood. I need the sense to smell for it and then
let it grow, except

my senses are misfiring in the domestic.

Imposition

*"There is no word for the 'floating' gender
in which we would all like to rest."*
—ANNE CARSON[1]

Not in the jam that sticks the lid.
Never under the thumb, the butter, kneading.

Not here on the shoulder do I know you, gender,
even though that's where you put your weight and pushed,

diminished me, left holes, some threads flagging the nail on the fence
that divides one from the other, as though there can only be two

sides at genital-height, rigid division. Not here
do you make longing out of absence. It sleeves on.

My adult voice careens through the house. I catalogue
spores and motes, things that dust my smallness

and can be wiped away with a finger, blown
up to settle somewhere else.

---

1 Carson, Anne. "Anne Carson, The Art of Poetry No. 88." Interviewed by Will Aitken. *Paris Review*, no. 171, 2004.

Wroxton, Saskatchewan

Bask in the summer of fathers dying.
     First your orchard, then my mother's

childhood: a place easy to imagine
     the both of us being but not all at once.

Before, your own past: some fruit stolen and driving
     drunk, angling the sound of the car toward

the lawn, headlights on your son and daughter's
     bedroom windows, and your wife hushing

you inside before straightening up your mess
     in case the neighbours could see the direction

of you. There, the small box of your life, that contained
     everything and so little of it.

After death: meeting for the first time, your grandness
     diminished and all your stories

sad. Even now, after all, there is no need to be ungenerous.
     We say what we can about ourselves.

If there is a word of mine you don't know, replace it
     but always for the better.

North of Nipissing Beach

I stood ankle-deep in polite water
and there was wind coming over the trees
and toward the camper where my mom and dad sat
with friends I only recognize
from one of their few wedding photos, by now out
of its frame and discarded. Under the surface,
my eyes darting little fish, so many and so quick,
moving in leafy patterns, an arrangement
that astounded. The memory astounds.
Laughter from behind me, cigarette smoke
and fire, an adult world where I was
a distraction, but here, ankles iced, such an enormous
and quiet childhood. And then that sudden moving
fish, two feet between mine,
making eights around me, colossal muscle
parting the water. It stayed until I called out, wanting
to be recognized by my parents for having been
chosen, but by the time
they set down their drinks, moved
from their folding chairs, the fish was gone, and moving
around me was the frustration of not being
seen. Even this memory is queer.
These are the terms of this space.

Sleep over

What shines through the shafts of memory:

flashlights
precise rows
nylon
polyester
wax
gymnasium
an older boy
beside
me

who has done this before.

Words need space between them

make form

am formal

polite.

Not an evasion, exactly,   but a way to breathe

in rooms with low light   many people, casual

contact, a way to tell   you instead

about my grandfather's garden,

where I think he kept a raspberry bush, how I might remember looking
down to a handful of berries all of them torn, that a lemon might
not leave my hands as sticky but it will sting them more, that I was
not hungry and that is why I pushed.

Where, the place to tell you what did happen:

Bathing

Under the boundary of water a knowing pulses

the skin. The condition of being made

to be human, that cruelty

wisping. Then: long dry garments to hide

a childhood. Learning what a body can do and then stripping

yourself of it. A young boy's wet brain talking

about the crudeness of the limb.

It becomes necessary to cover legs and arms

lest someone see you have them. For years

could not say the word *I*—could not

admit to being in a body, something fastened

to this world so tenuously, by the stretched thread

of skin that rots into creamy white fibres and breaks.

Behold another surface underneath, another body

that's kept secret from you. This is just the tip

of the nerve. First greeting depression in the incandescent dark

of bath time, wanting to be sick and wanting to be clean—

life bubbles up from the drain and cannot be emptied.

Kids in the back seat

A memory she tells me: my nervous childhood
stomach made sick by a prairie storm. Now in a space
on the other side and looking back
across the flat plain of before toward
the curved structure
of my small body writhing on the couch, surrounding
what I could not manage
to say. Growing up takes a little bravery
and that's all I had. She always had
more. She tells me about a drive
straight toward adulthood that I slept
through. Now, grown, how to follow
that long way back along the tire tracks
to where I left off? She was the other
passenger with whom I shared
a distance but not time. How to retrace
a relationship and then to stay present?
How to repair? I always push away
from the pain, but she reaches through and can see
me, can connect what I can't by a very long road.

Sister

For Nancy Lee
& Kelsey Purcell

Writes to me from a floor above,
from the other side of the photograph
where we keep looking up together.
Always separated by a handful of years.
Used to be so different—
a confidence and joy we all helped
snuff out. I could have been better
to the lost girls who live upstairs.
How do you walk back from that pain
and betrayal, the handprints, confess
your own violence and take back its effects?
You'd like to go back to that time
in the airport, when, after being separated
for only days, only two or three,
she runs straight for you
instead of away.

Talking to your first kiss on this side of death

The trees tonight cusping, a little lick

of the moon. I wish I hadn't just invoked the moon.

A little lick along a teenage memory, tentative, metal

on the tongue to taste the zipper. The trees tonight

rustling against the past as against a window, the wind

tonight smelling sweet and impermanent. Looking back

on what has hurt you knowing it is too late, doesn't matter. You

were hurt too, always trying to lift away from life. I knew then

that I would want it all back, the simplicity of the grass, the swing

swinging on its beam and the collision,

the landing, your cackle and love of danger. Flirting

for the first time with vanishing, with letting go.

I held tighter, so cautious, my trembling hand

against blue denim then beyond. An era

in a single evening: lilacs and laundry detergent

and underwear. The air with so much sleep

in it. Two boys and a whole world on the other

side of the door that only opens one way. I look

back now from that side, rustling against that past. I dismantled

my childhood, brought my bedroom window through

which to gaze at you, leaving a hole almost

twenty years wide, wide enough for the moon to fit in.

That moon again. It is not what I'm reaching for. What I'm reaching for

is a way to speak to you from across this distance, a way to pull

from my memory of you everything that poisons it,

what I've said to myself to keep me from saying

the truth, which I could say if only I could reach that evening.

Film of inexperience on the skin, my tongue shining

you for the first time. Even when you betrayed me, I stood

watch as you swung higher toward the end. I knew

it was a goodbye. It wasn't enough for me to want you. You wanted

me to fear you, an affect that holds tighter than love.

When I heard the news, I felt relieved, like I could finally

relax my hands. Then I was brought back here. You are just on the other side

of this life. What I would say if I could carry you

from the place you are now back here, back to this place, swinging,

where the air is heavy, swing you back awake for a moment to say

that we are connected and you are pulling me, swinging. We didn't have

to be enemies. We could have forgiven each other. The trees tonight

rustling against this space where it is

too late, where you are suspended mid-air and I am not.

Earring

Coming to return to your imprint, you, half
shadowed by lamplight. I'm scared of being a fag.

Your child coming home pierced, your voice
all the way through the wound

that never grows over. Where one can hang
things, the loop of silver, the ball, the night

heavy like an apple bending the bough, the bow
strung straight. But what if I am? A quiver

through the left lobe. We never could hear one another.
Perched on the side of your bed where I tried to be

understood as much as I understood myself
at that age and failing. Neither of us could move

beyond the syllable. It trapped us. I could not even say it
myself but you could see wounds all over me. O, here,

o, another, counting the spoiled fruit that is such a waste.
Time sharpened in all directions and still stays sharp.

A full apron at the side of your bed and nothing in it,
so much for us to inventory and barter over.

Finally, my father says, "Enough. All he wants
is to know that he can" and the long exchange ends

with us holding only what we brought in the first place. Nothing
has changed hands. We are both still wringing our fears.

A good father says, "You are my son," and reaches across
to touch the burning wound.

What seems worth evading

I can only pause on heterosexuality. You
remove the hair from your body at the door.
A footnote is useful for a citation or an aside. The
text is a mushroom. It rings deep underground

to the neighbour's yard. They are heterosexuals too.
It's odd that there are so many in this neighbourhood.
But there you go. I told them not to eat those mushrooms.
They said they'd put it in the newsletter. I feel

tenderness toward you. Some nights I know
you only posit heterosexuality. It is only two hands.
That's all we have been given. I have a desire. I grow
your body hair in a garden. You spread mostly underneath.

A predisposition and an event

the sleepy slap of depression
from a concept to a practice.

a practice of dropping
off the world and living on

where it is dark like dirt and cold.
a practice of excavating yourself

in a direction you can't sense.
how does the brain develop without sound?

that must be why i was drawn to you, seven years
my senior even when it wasn't legal.

you were older, free, above ground,
and i wanted to be lifted up. but then

you must have liked me below you and kept me
there. water poured down, all cracked.

walls swollen. my stomach
sick of holding what you showed to me.

and still i have made a life from down here, vining
toward the glint of adulthood. it is a straining upward,

a growing older than you like your boys
and still ruined roots rooted in the dark rot of you.

She fell

Her face turned toward me and hair fanned over
the neck like in sleep, moved by the wind, thrown
back in laughter, as though laid down
by love someplace soft and not by pain, here, this frosted
cement garage floor. Why when I stand toward love
do I only feel bones underfoot?

My eyes just
for show now—shame has filmed and dried them. I don't digest
that way anymore. I'm not the son I want to be. I am
the son that I am.

A glimpse of her hand curled on the tire moving me,
panning to reveal my fear to me, her thin body
perfecting limp angles that splice vision.

What do you do
with anger and love once they've yellowed? After
the table is cleared, the sound of vomiting quiets—a language
we both speak but never to each other. You are left
with yourself and it isn't until now, standing
left with yourself that you see you had no right to hold
against her all the things she could and could not swallow.
I don't want my love to be so violent.

Hit by the single bulb watching from above, one of us
shivers in the cold. Look again: the angle of the head, a serene
deception, and you think it would be so much easier
if it were always this quiet, in that groaning interval, where you are
again a sad little boy, waiting all night at the window for mother
to come home and to comfort you, to say she fell softly
while you kiss away the scrapes on her hands.

Simon and Vallier in the Tub

After Michel Marc Bouchard's Les feluettes

Finally, on page 60, Simon (clothed) jumps in after him
and the two lovers embrace. He has managed to speak
the word, arranged in a grammar

that empties me from the top. In Edmonton last fall:
the tub lit, Vallier's nude back turning the sound commodious,
more gay men seated around me

than this world has ever let me have. We flood the house
with a frisson of fingers on thighs, Adam's apples alight,
all throats swallowing together

protecting in our nervous stomachs a love that could kill us.
This opera, this Catholic education, the coifs worn beneath
habits, the shame we start fires over.

It would be nice to say that I have outgrown this fear of
being watched, disciplined, that the teenage judge of God
was only a feckless martinet, a dullness

to overcome. But instead, while two gay men embrace,
I worry that tub might rust, that something is always already
compromised, a violence about to transpire

off Vallier's roric skin. It occurs to me now how bathing
with my boyfriend wrung me like a sponge, my anxiety
filming the top of the water.

The tub is wheeled offstage with the two lovers inside.
If the moment of queer intimacy continues we aren't allowed
to see it. The pith of that realization

sticks to the skin, holds on to the teeth I used to scrape orange
peels at my childhood soccer games, where the white caught,
where he hit me when he found out.

Opposites

Boys pour out into an expanse of grass
                standing front to back fielding

in our deep dry oceans hot underfoot

                  and lonely.

I have had so many mothers I have been
                so many sons maybe

I ought to only have been one so it wouldn't hurt so much

to be pulled in these directions to be the one pulling.
                    I couldn't limit who made me. My palms

took everything held everything so gratefully and then

the way to feel it through the fingers is to let it go.
                    We wade through.

Childhood covering great distances and shadowing.
                    Only some of us can step through it

through its brightness, violet and loud, toward or away from our mothers.

Our mother's love
           something

I can't speak to, though she
           is in each word

and cannot be contained by them. I spill
        over in her language and cannot

please her. Her grammar
           trails behind me,

long grasses rustling dispersing as far

as you can look away. Her opposite is yours.

The shadow of her gaze her attention
         the inverse of a mother's love

is the problem.

It is what pulls you away from her, decentres her.

Living with the problem and fleeing it,
          crossing distance with both feet on the ground,

away from the flash and toward the sound of it.
        The sound of galloping.

A friend asks: what is the opposite of a horse? I say
        a rider.

A friend asks: who steered you this way? The only one
        who could.

'Berta Boys

After Kyle Terrence's 'Berta Boys[2]

a masculinity that cannot go further
the length of it more than its language
here, arms at the side and holding straight
down—forgetting
the lick that breezes over
smoke plumes, gravity makes itself known
over a scene, an absence, a way of being gendered
some unsound distance
smoking on the corner, pencil and then something darker
marking you, exposing you,
the weight of balls pulling you down toward
something you can't see
but that bruises nonetheless.

2 Viewed at Latitude 53, Edmonton, AB, May 18, 2019.

II
Sickness is not a metaphor.

It is what turns you into to a sickroom without power
              a flickering body, whirring
              toward activity and participation
              in spite of itself.
Pain is what interferes, what cuts up
                                        time
                                        attention
                                        language
so the mind is only half there while the body
              throbs its excess presence. It is what fragments
a life
with too much punctuation   sharp
intakes of breath that are held   the drag
of the semicolon across your clauses, its guts hanging
from the bottom of your tired voice ; that looks
like it's bleeding ; colon
from Greek *kōlon*, meaning limb,
                    that which can reach and hold
two independent ideas: that one can be sick and still
made   to participate in its own extraction
              production
interrupted
              sleep, conversations, thoughts.
The mind moves toward the minute, the particular,
the boring, all to keep the body in place, to return the world
              to a size that can be managed. Pain can be too big.

You make connections you would never make
in health. You see from the ground
                    what the well step over.
There is only enough of you
for the very small. You leave gaps in your logic
for those shafts of light to move through, dust dancing.
And when you record
the experience of your body you are not making sense.
That is not the language of pain.

Borscht

Lain horizontally and in thin slices, see that they have rings, that the harmed skin lifts itself, that they have left something on your hand that stays.

Blood in the toilet where you have thrown up a field, a swirling pot of steam.

Elimination diet

In secret separation
the yogourt's liquid semen
yellow pools sometime in the night,
bacteria straining under
the dark fridge light bulb, to be
spread on the tongue's morning
sick breath.

I ferment
outside the body / in jars /
on Instagram / lit by blue light
but not here,
in the ragged ropes of me,
which were infant strings once, too
delicate for breastfeeding.

The yeast overtakes the flora, flour
on my tongue smearing the lateral incisor.
Whatever converts to sugar in the body
flakes the skin to grey.
An animal in your water, their feet bound
in a little apple cider vinegar.
Pull out their collagen,

simmer their bodies overnight
their bones to salve the raw
wrecked wounds of your stomach.
Birth, the first bacteria, your tongue along
a seashell's ragged edge, its flesh sucked empty,
and you salivate over the toilet
seeing your teeth from the wrong side.

Cavity

The tooth runs so deep into the skull like a story.

The strongest thing can endure such grinding pressure
        until tiny holes form—

narrative inconsistencies betray the structure
        of what you tell yourself and the veneer

collapses. Broken teeth

have no teeth of their own with which to eat.

The healthy teeth do not either.

I guess what I want to know is what
        I'm trying to say.

One can only pull one's own tooth out if it is very loose.

You can wait for this to happen naturally (common
in the very young and very old), or you can use force.

You can pull your own truth from yourself, but what to do
with all the extra blood?

fertility

I pleasure over a row of white caps containing themselves. I tongue my
own holes. Dislodge a tooth with a filling in it and grind it out to see its
cavern, pushing against the walls of enamel with my thumb until the
entire structure of the filling crumbles. Gape it enough that it splits in
two, a thick rush of saliva on the tongue, alkaline and sweet. Holding my
own dead self in my hands. An artifact of neglect that rots and teems
with life. The slick of the mouth, its dirty floor mushrooming, iridescent
beetles just under the log, under the filling's wet dark suddenly lifted,
skeletal scuttling from the searching sun, from the rising dental light.

An appointment

The ordinariness of the molar

        sleeping under the   drill

jaw detached and tooth   emptied

        of pulp and nerve   roots

so long all the way into bone

        teeth go bad

from all the biting   rotted pain

          chewed and swallowed

and decaying between enamel

          spoiled breath

strapped in   under the   drill

roots   so long all the way

        to the brain

where you hope   they can extract

        the memory   and fill it

with something artificial

Cvetkovich's Teeth

The unspooling of the pain.
Use the first layer of skin to hold
the needle bouncing down the stairs of childhood
still carpeted, flossing with its fibres,
your tongue here measuring the pH of my mouth.

Baby tooth gouged and split right where the filling was, dead
dentin, cavity and a sick thrill from touching the sharp evidence
of my neglect toward my body in my hand, pressing its edge
into my skin until it cut through. A realization
that I let myself rot rather than nurture my aliveness, my belonging here.

Cvetkovich: taking care of one's teeth involves an act
of faith, the ability to believe that we can fix
what goes wrong and move on. But then the *persistent*
presence in my [m/d]*ental life* [is] *a reminder that I*
will continue to pay for my inability to take care of myself.[3]

3 Cvetkovich, Ann. *Depression: A Public Feeling*. Duke UP, 2012. 48.

bores through the teeth the jaw the mind
The mouth a container of health that I keep shut.
My joy dissolves in a pool of stomach acid
that has thinned me, my teeth soft and detached,
and I can only just keep myself from falling out.

Procedures for the end

In his hand a very small drill.
He will use it to grind away the enamel,
more than you would have wanted if you could
see, such a permanent reduction, exposing the
living tissue to the air for the first time, no autonomy
anymore as to how much of yourself is cut away
or what can find its way into you. But your eyes
are where they have always been. Portable electricity finds.

The whole head rattles. You do not grow
anymore. You get smaller and worse.
What you leave behind gets larger, harder to wash away.

A Diagram of My Teeth

The jaw locks like an account,
the disc of it skipping so that only
teeth 5, 6, 7 make contact
with the lower mandibular row
and it's true I cannot eat. I make
home in my body's restrictions.
I do not allow myself to chew. I hold myself
back from any food that could bore
into my teeth, jawbone, bloodstream,
that would make me carve away
the enamel that's left of me.
I suck away hunger, want to swallow
myself into the deep space of my stomach
an ulcered cavity no one's seen from the inside
but that I know intimately, can constellate.

Pain again

Strips the texture from the inner body,
a heat pouring then settling within the delicate
round cells that make you,
its thickness coating the places you can map
as intimately as the curve of a healthy body
beside you in bed, where you spend
most of your time now, stepping away
from the life that came before this.
Villi no longer dance like reeds.
This body heat dried them, this acid
water killed like coral.
You are so smooth now
where you shouldn't be smooth.
Nothing for your life to hold
on to. Only fantasies, thinking of your fingers
pushing through these ulcers,
stretching the holes until you come
through the other side. You slurp
along time and the wound lifts
exposing more of you
than you knew there was.

Grinding

Shirts mound along the wall bare
skin bent over rocking back and forth and clutching
the bath mat in both hands. Getting fucked
by pain kneeling and having to take it
all the way until it's finished. Jaw and joints
ache stretches the muscle with every flare the belly
bulging with every thrust in and out
the shape of it pulsing the sound
of moaning coming from somewhere—

swallowing is no use without the taste
or feel of acid everything
is preserved intact
grinding down the lip.

Men in the Gut

Scrape the inside of sleep the belly wall
tasting like yogourt cooked broccoli
the emptiness of the organ leaving its sour trace
on the tongue. Escaping the body
that wants to quit from the inside.
Your sick self unlaces you all the tethers sliced
away. When I dream of this body ending
of opening the germ of the pain
I am on the side of the road. My hands
hold out my stomach my second brain
to the men who already want me to die.
This failing organ, quivering stomach with a ruby
wound where everything settles
kissing your soft vulnerability your core
a target where it is so easy to be
stabbed or shot. A punch to the gut
I anticipate violence here one cell layer
deep shallow spreading roots
a memory system in my body.
On the side of the road a drive-by for men
homophobic in trucks swallowing spit.
When I was a teenager I let them
disembody me internalizing everything
through the mouth and now my stomach
wants it out. I am interested in self-
diagnosis. When I dream it is of trees

budding from my stomach
that will shade all the wounded men
who masculinity failed
who will lay their Oilers caps on my wrists
say *I'm sorry* and their fingers
will touch without their being afraid.

Waiting room II

Populated by sick patient spirits, a roll call of our hidden ailments from behind a partition. I blow into a tube that fogs. The nurse smiles absently while she fixes the stopper and files it away. Animals live in it now. Microbes homing against sterile glass grow and die in captivity. Someone will watch them from a critical distance and report that they were saved from a collapsing ecosystem, or that I am healthy after all. Back in the holding cell, a distant cough into the bored air.

Sleeping with House Guest

the vestibule of the mouth

        guests milling

        no room to even move the tongue

a whole new flora   licking

        fingers after turning sourdough   and

on the carpet of your gums   microbes dance

        or die

a duel   in the Russian winter   despite

        not being a novel   you imagine them

spinning   in their own dramas

         *

film develops   hangs   in the snoring dry

        darkroom

your cavity   you cannot pour into

it just takes a little light behind it to see

the way a dream does

how empty sirens are in sleep

and how sticky the smell

of morning

*

shuddering from your mouth after

a night of mushroom hunting   you spore

and hope some of them take   among the fallen

logs   and ferns   along the water

of your tired and   neglected gut

the acid yellowing the stony scar tissue   you go

down

with your hands full   and scattered

*

resting

a place only you know

you get there   by swallowing

carried down by pain   soft

furs on the water   the few that are left

and the ones who came

without your permission

they move so much faster

grow impatient   want to see

something violent   you cannot kill

a parasite at the root

Theatre of poor digestion

In the wings of your life you clutch at curtains
meant to conceal you. The fly system rigged to
the wound of your stomach, loads dead and alive
lifting like vomit, all over the lip and smearing
makeup. It is hard to enact belief when taking the stage
that life will get better   you have poisoned your mouth,
your shoes make a hollow sound.

Animal

The gut tissuing and hanging from the rafters
to dry, then to carry, that thing it's meant to do.

Pain licks the outline of my body where I live
only at the level of time, a unit of duration

and endurance. Under my hand another hand
cups the stomach, holds open a space

where these sensations are real—another hand
with interlocking fingers trying to keep human language

from falling while I groan from the teeth, pregnant
globes of saliva from the threads of my mouth

and the tectonic grinding of the vocal cords, articulating
that which is beyond thought, only body, only hands

holding me back from the deep toilet bowl, where I might drink
a taxonomy that will dehumanize me to the healthy.

In the wide maw of the world: a precarity of bacteria,
a leather bowl of cream, the animal, starved and limping.

fur

Would rather be draped
suspended whispering cell structure
the skin doesn't need the organs below
gets by without the stomach the lungs
only its attractive outsides silked
and coiffed to shudder under fingertips
writhing from pleasure pain
no longer animating the frame
a desiring subject to be filled
finally able to be used and not
so gentle
only a faint vinegar fume on the breath
a chemical affect betraying the hollowness
of this taxidermy all the unpleasantness
of decay cut away I live a longer life this way
moving into me fist to elbow, wear me.

Filling

I can taste
    without filling my mouth,

my full throat deep
    down and the place it finishes

bulging, all without
    swallowing anything I can feel

molars sting, dark
    holes appear and begging

to be filled,
    grinding and shaped

as before, and resilient,
    though not as strong as

bone. All these things
    I do without doing them

but am left with the effects,
    the abrasions and erosions,

the tunnelling
    and the expense. All that sugar

syrup dripping
	and sticking to the unconscious,

following through
	the day, on every surface, until

the jaw hurts and keeps
	hurting, a bee in the mouth,

a finger that probes,
	that tickles and pricks

and presses down
	against the swelling,

where I am bursting
	and he gives me a pop

and a warning,
	too much cum could rot

your teeth, and a candy
	something sweet to suck on

on the walk back home,
	to fixate on until the next visit.

If in coloured glass

From the teeth, a short distance to the skin.
  Gently, so gently, lower yourself onto desire
  that conifers, your prick
  seeding preposterously.

My swollen belly full of meal
  local honey to introduce me to the pollen
  of this place, so good
  for wounds the fingers.

Under high heat turns to glass
  a hardness of the tear ducts;
  nothing religious, but a bruise of masculinity
  the size of the pit when the fruit is gone.

River Poem

The dipping white spruce, the cold
morning kept from me by sheets
of glass. The whole world out there attached
        to the whole world.

Water falls from my open mouth. I cough
out nothing. I want to drink through
the hands, feeling everything
        through a little tube in the vein.

Retire the mouth. It is too complicated.
Where I floss the night from my teeth, where I pull
the grit from the throat fist by fist, where I watch
        the vomit drip back into the mouth.

Anyway, I am too dry to be a site of pleasure.
Sourness tapes the touch. Anyway, I am mostly time
now, and less of it more and more. Anyway,
        it isn't very interesting.

I want a very nice nurse. I want to go
down to the river, still iced over but opening up
in slices. I want to slip in among the dipping white
        spruce and then under.

Recovery

Move so delicately along the grooves

beneath the skin, on the underside,

the ribs, the shoulder blades, the spine,

wear away the soft generosity and care,

extensions of love that bend like ligaments.

Affects flare and transfer between bodies

so that the one who is sick touches the other

and both tire. Everything shows its mark.

The loss of small things: holidays, nights out, dinners with friends,

and the arrival of medication, heating pads, long nights

in bed without intimacy.

Both try to create the conditions for wellness,

ignoring the permanent grooves in the couch,

the stains   from the wrong kind of sweat,

the smell   of bad health kept too long in one room.

Both think   they can endure the conditions of this life

while repairing   the daily strain they share until

a snap   from the bond connecting their bodies

and they are left   with marks on their bones

their muscles   stringing all the way down and trembling lines

toward their separate hands   suddenly open and empty.

Magpie

One magpie rustles in the shine

      wet bacteria between my skin and clean shirt

the space between

                concealment and nudity

the lives I am carrying on my chest

I can't see

a corner   hesitant

      along Jasper Avenue, long

time to wait in the summer dust

         full patios blooming with car exhaust

      gravel in the teeth

through the cracks are more cracks

      and the threat of your tongue

caws at your bad jeans

you look straight

across the moment toward no destination

ten blocks to your apartment

you shoulder me

toward   repellant metal
                refusal

your
desire is an engine

that motors   an idea good or bad toward collision
that eats   with its hot teeth what is offered   what is not
that spits   up its waste and trails it through the streets
that stalks   across healthy plains springing oil
that occupies   bedrooms boardrooms   for fucking

pedestrian fantasies   following you because I am caught

in sociality and commerce   in a body

sweating sympathetic apocrine warning

lights on   the first inoculation

          by your tongue, the bacteria of your mouth

moving in mine   frantic and impossible

               to remove now   swallowed
                                                by reflex
                                                without consent

the liquid you expel   drips

          from your skin into the hollow

of my clavicle   and teems

          in the morning, sticking to you   and peeling

               your salt and oil away

to step out into the spilling sun   to escape

to somehow wash away your intrusion

lift from my chest
fifty pounds
of your bacterial weight
and breathe again

and clear away your body deposits that shine me, attract birds.

III
If I had a window, it would be open.

We approach the end. We look out.
The future has slowed, rocked off course
by a protrusion, a bundle of clothes, a deep cavern
the earth did not want and teeters
right at the wrong edge.
The world's fluids wet the surface. We drink. We don't
have many choices before us. We go on
toward tomorrow's many edges,
tonguing the rim.

                    Or, we can say the pain stops.
           We can say this world, what's left of it, is for us.
                 We have learned to make life, to walk
        long distances, to be together, to coax from the rubble
                              a sign of life.

villa

A housefly had the misfortune of dying so indecently. Part of it separated, itself next to itself. When sliced open its blueberry greenness glistened and oozed. It was time for lunch, you said suddenly, and you were hungry.

On Acicular Ice

How the cavity of the body, when poured into
improperly, does not heal or offer
the satisfying sensation of fullness, but instead opens up further
opportunities for emptiness. Nothing buries deeper. Fault
lines connect, infrastructure for survival
collapses. The hairline fractures.

In plain language: I have kept my queerness
locked inside the body. Objects
in my mirror. It goes deeper
inside than it appears from out. A very long fist
can be lost. Turn the body inside out and it goes
on for days; choose length or depth. A secret
under the skin can unfold forever—search it:
your gloved hand beaking. Hold it
as I have, like a leashed animal, or an ashamed boy
wading in the mire of his first self-consciousness, waiting
in a parking lot, and it wastes away. It comes
through the teeth anyway, ruins the stomach wall, creaks through
like bad circulation. You've done this to yourself but of course,
no, you haven't.

Acicular ice firms at the border
of established ice and water on the verge, long tunnels
of crystal that bubbles pass through. Spaces of transition
between states offer a kind of hope: I could
refuse to carry this fear inside another day. This could
happen all around me, acicular ice tubing along
the skin and the outside world giving a new shape, defining
the dimensions of my new body, the old mould I stuffed
my queerness into, a cavern
with fingers to be caved in on.

Zellers

The music video for "Doctor Blind" by Emily Haines & the Soft Skeleton, the relic I return to, its red sticky linoleum line, the buzz of the high yellow lights, the canned footfalls in my ears, the plastic hangers shrieking across the bending metal rack by now smothered in some landfill. In the St. Albert Zellers beside the Neilson chocolate rosebuds where I learned my drama teacher had died from cancer of the stomach. You lose touch after death. I don't know now whether she is underground or burned up and breathed in. This place, its grey artificial air and its thick restaurant milk, felt liminal, a train stop on the way to the end, where I would follow a straight boy following the girl he wanted believing that desire only ever ran its tracks in one direction, where time and hope fell flat against each other. Now that this place is gone and the end of the world is all around us, the air outside desaturated, and now that I don't want to be here anymore, my own stomach counting down, it feels like the only familiar place, where I am able to return on repeat, reaching through my laptop screen, slipping in to the background of Haines's video, becoming one of the falling figures in rigid rest, making bed in its aisles, looking past my dark bedroom straight through the lines of lights to the bats in the rafters.

The smoke

Hearing your strained lung smoked out
in this asthmatic season that follows the last, follows
us everywhere, seeping in between the cracks
in our fingers, over our eyes. I listen to you pull
air with both hands
through the stones in your lungs, drag
it in its new dimension, solid, with taste
of brown snow, like the air had been rolled
in the gutter. There is fire at every distance
and clouds move out toward the edges, a fascination
of air. Movement plumes, ashes decline, you walk
slower through this, your lungs ejecting the residue
of calamity. You have to be careful. There are
no hospital beds left in Alberta. We seal the windows,
not realizing we've trapped a small beetle between
glass and plastic. It shows its wings, darts and is stopped
by two transparencies, preserved in a liminal world,
suffocated by crisis in two untenable directions.

A list of symptoms

The dirty rivers, shopping carts in the spleen, oil
in the pores, microplastics, plastics of any kind, that sting
when I wash the dry flaking
earth, red and sore underneath as it is above,
inflammation all through the woods, the sky's collapsed
lungs wheezing, hot heavy heat wave air puddling
on the splitting sidewalk stuffed
with abandoned stems and dehydrated worms,
bleeding from so many wounds, drinking that blood,
burning that blood, turning that blood into plastic
of any kind, bones collecting in the watershed,
bones with two heads, frogs unable to leap,
swim, not far from the treetops: smokestacks,
reactors, communities being poisoned,
radioactivity snowing from the air,
cars exhausting and sleep
pressing down on the skull like the printless finger
of the doctor hunting
for a reason to be sick.

inadequate insurance

The gender of climate emergency, ferocious whiteness
as white as capital in the mouth, a currency.
I too walk with the economic privilege of debt
weighing me. Indebtedness, a consequence

of living. Having to perform your own extraction,
suck up your own oil, claw out your own coal,
grind your own tooth all the way through the nerve
and wipe the blood from your own infected gums,

and then pay for it all and keep paying.
What it costs can vary. You can pay for hands
in the mouth. You can pay for interference
with your body, to fix a problem you were designed

to inherit. Your body mishandled from birth,
left alone in a broken soiled cradle. Watch
as the wounds are washed
with water, boiled so it's safe, the water table

smashed and polluted, inverted rainbows slicking
the crust of lakes and oceans, black glass
on the feathers, in the gills, bubbling raw
intestines of those whose lives are not

grievable. Having to pay for your own debasement
with the last of your pride, then crawling
back to your people: the hollow-toothed,
crooked fingers interlocked, who have

waited for you to return, stitched together
their empty pockets into a blanket
with which to wrap you so you are at least
warm while you bleed.

Too late

The climate of the gut. What is coming. Nodes acid away layer after layer. Fertile earth degrades. One lifetime of topsoil to live with and a millennium until it's replenished. The torn mucosal barrier. The hole in the sky. Soon the sun will get too close. I look backwards, as though this world is a memory: a magnifying glass, the sun, a patch of dry grass, the coil of the heating pad on all our bodies. Our hands are burning, forcing up its throat, fingering the hole until it's so wide we can see the fire below. Acid climbing up the throat the way a fire licks the fuse. The body wants to cough but it hurts most on the inhale. Looking at its details through that magnifying glass, the line of hot ruin sweeping the forest like a name.

Not in your lifetime

She crossed the street at a diagonal. The roads sliced up the land where it was not meant to be sliced. These are settler lines.

Hot white lights broke the night above her, an advertisement for a discount airline, and even higher are trails from the new Amazon planes touching down in Edmonton three times a day. The local is a myth. We live in a corporation.

The seasons brush against her face, no longer in their own time but in ours; rain falls in December. She burrows her hands into a downtown planter. Nothing is frozen.

She feels the change on the wind and in the water, in her mouth, a still house of death that creaks. She passes another person, a man, his eyes coated in plastic and cast downward toward his phone, who hurries past into a parkade. Otherwise the sidewalks are empty. The road is empty. This is not a place for people anymore.

She remembers the warnings, the urgency and the refusal, the care and the neglect. She remembers gender. She remembers the future. She remembers everything that doesn't matter anymore, perhaps never mattered. She goes on.

Some of us broke some of us

In the middle of the night, the hand hives.
I said to my friend
—   a slippage of conversation
—   desire moving against the ear, the sound of outside coming in; in
         what space do they meet?

And then, the ruckus.
And then, the

pouring sand onto the earth. There is so much movement
below the concrete, so much of it must be
pulsing, as when

the cast is on and you itch.

Having a body in the petrostate

that which clarifies
an embarrassment of nerve endings

tongues grimed
all the way from fort mcmurray

in bouncing barrel chests
brimming

a body that was mine and is now
a burden

only mine, a secret
overgrown pickups with truck nuts

as big as they can get them
one by one in a line

each one topping the one who came before
all lubed up with oil and bent

bad backs from the hard
work of shouldering this culture

(all the way to the shoulder)
on their delicate bodies

broken but for a good wage.
drinking until sick,

sick until drinking, sick
because their bodies are crushed

by bad sleep and bad air, fumes
and a view down into hell,

so they deserve this, okay?
a little joyride, a little pleasure

before they're too sick and broken
to call themselves alive anymore.

down the long road, the city's ring

rimming the suburbs,
a little secret joy.

thirst

To talk about it as something that occupies me
a thought, a fixation
militarized, violence that can cross the mind
and find there are no limits to its movement

to this astringent night. A bed frame periods.
You wake like Christmas for an intravenous,
dry throat clichéing the depression you seek
like a small animal, find in your pillow

a long hair like the one you could have grown,
that your body has prepared to grow. Scalp
woken in the night from its wet sleep by noise
outside. By your ears. Your inner ear streets.

You simply want to be. You simply want. Not
the angled pain of hair through the skin.
An acquaintance with blades. A brand
of underwear. It is hard to believe. You even, your evening, this.

So many genders use their voices.
So many through the window.
The screen has so many holes for them.
A scream has so many holes.

a word like guilt

Where our homes are
governed, inners and uppers,
responsible for the cooling of my apartment
by means of destruction.

One of us breathes.
Shirts can be mesh, linen.
So much milk glass before the heat
curdled, needing conditioning,

that is to say, I'm afraid nothing will grow
in this space between windows. It is more
or infinite, this cannon sound. The click
of the world. Summers will be hot. Winters too. Consider

the house itself. The floor buckles from all this
melting. The house shouldn't be here at all.
We shouldn't be here at all, with our
itchy molars, our hands fleshing the ground,

our bodies in body holes. We are mouthing anger
that the world will be taken from us
the way we took away the world.
Look how limp we forward.

only beginning to question

Begin with what is formulaic and normative
a command, that twists the language
by its nipple, a noise that comes from
three mouths

my gender; my occupation; my sleep

erupts me in darkness
where I am leaving, you see
how many more leaves here than before
rushing up toward a climate
roundly

if I were to stretch my arm through this space
if I were to stretch
my arm through this space and then
the hair toes
a line a line a line, all of them lining
skin touched by gender
ad nauseam.

Long shadows

The married men on my street are getting hotter. It is unbearable. Climate changing in their yards, in their second-floor bedroom windows, where they are fogging up the whole block. Watch their eyes as they cruise down the street, adjusting their collars.

Seeing as these are end times, it would be best if we all agreed to stop pretending. Put the lawn mowers away, give the wildflowers one last chance. Stop salting the winter walks around the arthritic trees stroking our last frosts.

Stop the unnecessary work and let our bodies heal, feel joy, feel pleasure, these affects we haven't been allowed. Take back our ground down teeth and bones. Stop using what's left of our muscle to press against crumbling walls; use them to hold another body, and another, and another.

Open your doors and pour out your desire into the street so that it takes the shape it's meant to, so that it mixes with all else, so that you can finally see it in the light.

danse macabre

We dance together lengthwise through the night.
Its long violet distance curls up in front of us like a hair
over a flame, turning to hard carbon, smelling
like the earth will smell when we get to the end.
We already know, those whose bodies have already seen time
shrivel in front of our feet, burn up,
what is happening. We know, those of us
who have had our bodies pressed against inevitability,
that the world is following suit in its slow crackling
orange way. This world that has maligned
our deviant bodies is ending, and we dance
our sick disabled dance, carrying each other
past the shaking lights of refineries and the deep pits
of derricks, away from the cavity white world of extraction
in a line that spans beginning to end, linked by our hands
and a refusal to mourn the end of this. We dance toward utopia,
the place we are forever returning to,
to be embraced, told to rest, that old song is over.

a bed

A bed that faces up.
An invention that needs no alternative.
The air rises that way when heated, which was to be the future of air.

A bed that is not a sickbed.
A bed that waits for pleasure, for bodies that stretch,
that yawn because they are rested.

A bed that is made crisp,
that is cool, that is for holding, that keeps safe in the night,
that dawns.

Ceramics with Emily

For three hours it is only the hands that move. The wedging of the clay draws from the shoulders and the chest, wrists already in their memory. You, with your knitting injury, at it again. Jointing fragility. It is only three hours. The hands move. It is the clay that reaches out to be held, where it is warmed, hum the notes behind the notes.

Ceramics with Emily II

Of course, you are immediately proficient. While I thumb the clay into something I hope will hold together, you have rolled a pot and lid, rolled it with total attention and precision until it is perfectly smooth. Rolled it until your palm, using only the slightest force, only what force is necessary, and the gentleness that is necessary too.

Sourdough with Emily

i have a question for you:
would you consider ours a queer friendship?

i.
Baking for me:
The scene of cradling the dough, inflated
and taut, a belly put down to rest
in its bed basket, towel-lined,
to watch while it sleeps.

ii.
You talk about being a mother.
You are made of care, an ecology
of thoughtfulness tender on your hands
folded in. Half of you in the inside,
half of me too.

iii.
Moving to London, a new biogeography.
It was grad school and neither of us
were well, our guts nor brains nor
hungry hands. Microbial exchanges touch
in long-distance time, dough lifted over.

iv.

Over the *field*[s] *of intimacy*
love just grows wild—Eve Sedgwick.[4]
Becoming a family. Break bread, share bacteria,
where I reciprocate care for you,
love on gut-level.

4   Sedgwick, Eve. *A Dialogue on Love*. Beacon Press, 1999. 214.

My gender

A cookbook half-open on the couch
that blows the soft herbs drip in sensual memory
coming hither on the teeth

the way the coconut and its milk
announce themselves exactly as they are
its solids on the fingers.

I would like to substitute myself
thoughtfully, as when forgetting
to pick up cilantro and so basil instead

infusing the meal
at the last minute, when it all seems
like it could be too late,

a little change, a swap, into the same but—
It's silly to make this into an equation,
but here, scribbled on the counter

as I cook dinner for only myself,
no one here to see how I stir,
how I adapt what I've been given,

the recipe as it should be, and fine that way,
and how I've always been   taught to eat it,
but then to learn I prefer this other way.

ruinous women

Because in the footprints
of ruinous women rainwater
floods & throats sing

& we are held by ruinous women.

Surviving in my queer body
only because of ruinous women
generations of genders accumulate

& stitch care up & down time, a return.

All the women I know
& love have ruined something
for the better / ruined me

for the better, made openings.

The best parts of this world
are the women who want to ruin it
so fiercely and attentively

gutting it with their starter & scoby.

It is laughter from the future,
finally the sound
of the other side of shattering.

in the garden with my faggots

who teach me to laugh with each of my teeth,
to pearl them among the pansies, to pluck
from my brows the masculinity i have covered
my vision with, to line my eyes
with wrinkles, who i sit with
and nourish myself with what we've grown:
chard and radish and mint, to heal
with honey and hot broth.
who help me return to the comfort
of proximity to bodies, of belonging
to bodies, to a chorus of voices that includes mine,
gathered in mounds of blankets
and draped in smoke, to breathe in,
to love that i am alive.

ACKNOWLEDGMENTS

This collection was written in amiskwacîwâskahikan, Treaty 6, my favourite place on Earth.

My heartfelt thanks to the editors of the publications that gave a home to earlier versions of some of these poems: *Glass Buffalo*, PRISM *international*, *Contemporary Verse 2*, and the *Mulahat Review*.

Poems from this collection have also previously appeared in *A Place More Hospitable*, published by Anstruther Press. Thank you to Jim Johnstone for seeing something in my poetry and helping to shape that collection and so much of what followed.

"Cvetkovich's Teeth" quotes Ann Cvetkovich's *Depression: A Public Feeling* (Duke UP, 2012).

The epigraph to "Imposition" quotes an Ann Carson interview by Will Aitken in the *Paris Review* (no. 171, 2004).

"Sourdough with Emily" includes an altered quotation from Eve Sedgwick's *A Dialogue on Love* (Beacon Press, 1999).

My deepest gratitude to everyone at Arsenal Pulp Press for believing in this book: Brian Lam, Robert Ballantyne, Cynara Geissler, Jaiden Dembo, and Catharine Chen. It has been a dream come true to work with you on this book. Thank you to Alison Strobel for proofreading. Jazmin Welch, thank you for giving this collection shape and form with your design and layout and for seeing it so fully.

Joshua Whitehead, for guiding me through these poems, for pushing me toward precision and specificity, and especially for your friendship. It has been a joy and an honour to work with you on *Swollening*. Thank you.

My unending thanks to Alex Dimitrov, Leah Horlick, Vivek Shraya, jaye simpson, and K.B. Thors for providing such generous readings of *Swollening* and for offering such kind blurbs. It means so much to be in community with you and I am inspired by each of you.

Zachary Ayotte, for knowing my angles and what I need to read next.

Kyle Terrence, for '*Berta Boys*.

Marie Carrière, Keighlagh Donovan, Emily Hoven, Jessica Johns, Emily Riddle, Matthew Stepanic, Karyn Wisselink, for the conversations about books and writing, more for the laughter and friendship.

Justin Bilinski, for everything.

Photo credit: Zachary Ayotte

JASON PURCELL is a white settler writer from Treaty 6 territory. They co-own Edmonton's Glass Bookshop.